Lord, It's Me Again

ALSO BY ALTON H. WILSON:

SO . . . HELP ME, LORD

Lord, It's Me Again

Alton H. Wilson

DOUBLEDAY & COMPANY, INC.
GARDEN CITY, NEW YORK
1975

Library of Congress Cataloging in Publication Data

Wilson, Alton H
    Lord, it's me again.

    1. Prayers. I. Title.
BV245.W49   242'.8
ISBN 0-385-09626-7
Library of Congress Catalog Card Number 74-22842

INTRODUCTION

Not many people call me "Papa." Only my two girls. And I love it. I rarely tire of hearing their call, because they are my children. But the Heavenly Father *never* tires of hearing His children. He never wearies of our prayers, whether they be praise or petition.

The Psalmist, in this confidence, bared his heart to his God. In Psalm after Psalm, he exulted, rejoiced, wept, and agonized in prayer. He shared every form of human experience with his Creator, and his prayers have blessed mankind ever since.

Men pray for two reasons. They either do not know God, and cry out in their efforts to find Him, or they have found Him, and call out to Him because He is their Father. I pray because of the latter.

The greatest affirmation of my faith is that my heart cries out to my Heavenly Father. The Scripture says, "And because ye are sons, God hath sent forth the Spirit of his Son into your hearts, crying, Abba, Father." (Galatians 4:6) "Abba" is an Aramaic term of endearment meaning "daddy" or "papa."

"The heart has its reasons, which reason knows nothing of," said Pascal, the French philosopher. That is especially true of prayer. Why pray? The heart demands it. The heart cannot live without it. The heart prays automatically, constantly, and lovingly, because it has its own reasons.

The reasons for *Lord, It's Me Again* are found in the prayers themselves. Each was born in a moment of need, a time of crisis, or an experience of worship. Some of the prayers relate to my family life, but most revolve around my personal spiritual relationship with my Heavenly Father . . . my Abba, Father.

If these prayers are poetic, that is incidental. They are primarily prayers. Personal, intense, and meaningful to me. As they find their way to you, my reader, I hope they strike a common chord in your heart. If so, maybe you will say, "Why, that's how I feel, Lord." And you will have prayed.

Lord, It's Me Again

1.

Lord, it's me again!
I sometimes wonder if You are wearied
By my continual coming to You . . . and more . . .
If You are distressed by my constant need to come.
Thank You, Lord, that if it does bother You,
You have never been impatient about it,
Nor have You ever failed to listen.
It seems I am always coming to You
Again . . . and again . . . and again.
But then that is what grace is all about,
Isn't it, Lord?
Grace is an ever open door, an eternal entree
Into the presence of One who can meet the needs
Of we who are always consumed with needs.
There are times I am tempted not to come,
Fearful that You may tire of me,
Or lose patience or simply be too busy.
I know better, for You have invited me to come.
Come boldly, You say.
Come quickly, You say.
Come now, You implore.
Come again, You intreat.
So . . . it's me again, Lord.
No big need.
No big deal.
Just me, coming to You,
Longing for Your fellowship, Your presence,
The assurance of Your continued love and forgiveness.
It's me . . . Your child,
Seeking the warmth and comfort and love
That only my Heavenly Father can give.
Thank You, Lord,

That in Your infinite grace, You have said
That I am to come to You,
Again . . . and again . . . and again.
So . . . it's me again, Lord.

Lord,
May I never lose a sense of wonder.
The wonder of life,
Of love,
Of beauty,
Of joy,
Of health,
Of nature,
Of wonder itself.
The thrill of childhood is that there is a wonder
In all of life.
The tragedy of growing up is that wonder is lost,
Step by step as we progress toward maturity,
Until one day it is seemingly gone
Beyond recall,
Almost beyond remembrance.
Thank You, Lord,
That You give a sense of wonder to life again.
With You, all things are new and fresh
And a radiance is brought to life
That is dulled and departed otherwise.
I thank You today, Lord,
For the sense of wonder I find
In the myriad redbuds in profuse bloom,
The dogwood gracing the landscape
In touches of white elegance;
The bluebonnets blooming in vast fields of splashy color,
The Indian paintbrushes stretching mile after mile,
Interspersed with lush burgundy wild clover;
For the good fresh earth
As it turns into softness at the touch of the pitchfork
Preparing it for the summer garden.

It's spring, Lord,
And I am held again in the wonder of it all.
I am reminded of life,
The promise of immortality
Of which Your resurrection was the earnest of mine,
Of ours.
Oh, my Lord,
May I never become so sophisticated
That wonder is rendered impossible.
May I so live in Your presence
That wonder will be the essence of life.

Lord,
This one thing I know.
You are the righteous judge of all the earth.
Whatever I may see, or think, or feel, or experience
That would lead me to think contrary,
You will do only that which is right and good.
My mind can never solve, even to my own satisfaction,
The mysteries of injustice, disaster, death, disease, poverty,
Or the myriad things in life
To which there is no plausible reason.
I cannot fathom the death of babies,
Millions dying of starvation,
Earthquakes, floods, pestilence, famines.
Like millions who have gone before me,
Pondering the mysteries of the universe,
No logical explanation has ever been sufficient
To soothe the troubled seas
Or still the tempests of the mind of man.
There is no answer.
Save one.
Faith!
Not faith in the abstract.
Not a faith without an object,
But a faith that behind it all
Lies the goodness and greatness of an Almighty God.
Unless there is this faith, Lord,
All *is* senseless and cruel.
There would be no hope—only darkness and fury.
But I thank You, Lord,
That You have stilled the storm
In the heart that is filled with faith.
You have given sense to an otherwise senseless existence.

The questions still come.
The doubts still linger . . . sometimes more than ever.
Yet, underneath, there is the placid assurance
That being God, You can be trusted
To bring order out of chaos,
Light out of darkness,
And, as the judge of all the earth,
All You do, or let happen, is good and right.
So, Lord, in faith I trust . . .
Until faith becomes sight.

4.

Abba . . . Father!
My heart cries out to You,
Because I am Your son.
And, because I am Your son,
You, my Father, have placed deep within my soul
The longings and yearnings and cravings
For deeper fellowship with You.
You have placed within me Your Spirit
Which causes me to cry out "Abba . . . Father."
It is really Your Spirit crying out.
Oh, Lord!
The miracle of Your Spirit in me.
There was a time I did not long for You
Because I was not Your son,
Because Your Spirit did not indwell me
And could not cry "Abba . . . Father."
But when You found me . . .
When I became Yours,
Not only by creation but by purchase,
There was placed deep within the recesses of my being
An insatiable hunger and thirst
Which is at once both a craving and a satisfaction.
It is when I do not hunger and thirst
That I die inwardly.
My very longing for You is evidence I belong to You.
Abba . . . Father!
You are my life, my joy, my all.
I cannot live,
Nor do I want to live
Without the yearning after You
Which is my assurance that
I am Your son,
And You are my "Abba . . . Father."

5.

Lord,
He asked me how I could be so sure,
How I could prove what my heart tells me is so,
That You arose from among the dead
To be my ever-living Lord?
My answer, nearly bursting from deep within
Seemed so paltry when placed against his claims
That science and reason have eliminated You.
I was no match for his brilliance, Lord.
I could not deftly fend his intellectual darts,
Nor reason with a logic cold.
I could only answer with the heart
That which I cannot prove by tangible evidence.
In my lackluster, simple way,
I could only speak of that which I know of You.
I know where I was before You found me.
Purposeless, alone, desperate.
But You brought meaning, peace, and joy,
Which neither wealth nor wisdom could bring.
To my darkened world You brought light.
To my loveless soul You brought love.
To my labored heart, rest,
To my warring mind, peace.
I cannot prove You, Lord.
Not to him. Not to anyone.
But I can be sure. I *am* sure.
For when You came into my life
It was a homecoming.
A release.
A rest.
A peace.
A joy.

A fulfillment
The world has never been able to give
To the philosopher, the scientist,
The religious, the pious.
Because You live, I live.
Because You arose from the dead,
I too shall live eternally.
How can I be so sure?
As sure as east becomes west,
As night turns to day,
As youth becomes age,
So sure am I
That God raised You, Jesus, from the dead
To be my ever-living Lord,
And thus, I too shall live.
The heart has reason to be sure.
Alleluia! Alleluia!

6.

Lord,
The fig tree was barren.
It bore no fruit.
Only leaves.
When You came looking for food
It could give You nothing but leaves.
Barren . . . fruitless . . . unyielding.
You pronounced a curse on the tree
And it died . . . immediately,
Forever a mute testimony
Of a missed opportunity
To minister to the Son of God.
Lord, I am startled by Your action.
It almost seems unfair
Until I remember . . . You created the tree.
You had every right to expect
A savory meal of figs to satisfy Your hunger.
Even if it were not the season
For the tree to have fruit,
It ought to have borne it for its Creator.
It failed.
It did not fulfill its purpose.
It withered and died.
Justifiably.

Thank You, Lord,
That You do not treat me so.
Thank You for the lesson You were teaching.
Help me not to miss the point
That You expect more of me than the tree,
For You have told me I am the branch,
Connected to the life-giving Vine.
In complete union, without struggle,

I may bear the fruit of Your likeness
So that others may feed on Your grace.
A natural process, simple, uncomplicated.
Attached to You, the Vine,
I can quietly, effortlessly bear fruit,
Fulfilling Your purpose for me.
Detached, I will wither and die,
For my life comes from You.
Apart from You there is no life for this branch.
Oh, Father,
Thank You, that in grace
You have not cursed me
Or caused me to wither and die
When I have been so like the fig tree.
Help me, Lord, that I shall not be barren.
May I let Your life flow unhindered through me
To effect fruit that will honor You
And succor others.

Lord,
The house is hushed.
The children are asleep.
My wife is in bed, probably reading.
It's quiet now, after a long, hectic day.
The embers in the fireplace flicker softly.
The stillness is soothing and serene.
There's peace here, Lord,
As I reflect all alone on this good day.
Thank You for the warm glow of heart and hearth.
Thank You for the haven of home,
A place to relax after a work day,
And the sense of security it gives
Just to sit here and ponder, to savor
The richness of home, of love, of family.
Simple things all.
But unrivalled, unmatched, unequalled
By all else this world has to offer.
How rich I am.
How blessed I am.
How secure I am,
For in it all, You are the center,
The circumference, the hub
Around which this home turns.
I pray it may always be so.
Bless my sleeping family, Lord.
I pray You will give to them
A portion of the joy and contentment I know
In this still moment.
Thank You for these quiet times
In the sanctuary called "home."
These times that prepare us for the onslaught of the world.
My heart cries "Abba . . . Father."

Lord,
I thank You, today,
That when I need to hide
You are my hiding place.
The storms of life always come,
Forcing us to find a place of refuge and comfort.
The fierce battles we fight deep inside
Make it necessary to withdraw
To a place of retreat, protection, and safety.
Thus, Lord, You are my hiding place.
The dog-eat-dog world of materialistic competition
Crowds us to the brink of physical and emotional chaos.
Then, Lord, You become my hiding place.
A hiding place in which I may
Shut out my world, my problems, my fears,
My loneliness, my distress, my temptations,
And rest securely in the place of refuge,
Sheltered and covered,
Protected and loved.
For You, Lord, are my hiding place.
I am not ashamed to hide.
There are times when not to hide
Would be utterly foolish.
I am not too proud to hide
For I readily admit life is too big for me
To face alone, unaided.
I pity those, Lord, who have no hiding place.
They can never retreat
For those times of refreshing that come from You
That make it possible to go back into an alien world
To face life, with all its demands,
Unafraid and with courage.

Like the Psalmist who had a secret place
Where he lived under the shadow of Your wing,
I too abide in peace and quietness,
In safety and protection,
For You, Lord, are my hiding place.
There is no other place, no other retreat,
No other spot of safety.
All else is vain.
All else is false.
All else is vulnerable and unprotected.
Thank You, Lord,
That You are my hiding place.
    I rest. . . .

9.

Lord,
I pray for my missionary today.
I have never seen her,
But we are friends,
And my heart reaches out to hers
Across thousands of miles
To the cold, wind-swept, icy Alaskan island
Where she lives, and serves.
She is middle-aged, Lord.
A woman alone in that barren land.
She chops her own wood for heating and cooking.
She cuts slabs of ice and carries them to her cabin
For her water supply.
I've only heard them talk about her at church.
She is on our prayer list this week, Lord,
And I have thought about her,
Prayed for her all week,
Wondering if she must not be lonely,
Or ill, or hungry.
If so, Lord, bless her.
Help her know there are those who care,
Who remember . . . who pray.
Why would a woman give up the "normal" life
Of home and comforts
For a life like hers?
There can be only one reason, Lord!
She has found her life
By giving her life to You
And to others.
I pray for my missionary friend, Lord.
Bless her real good today.

10.

Lord,
Like the Prodigal Son
Who, when awakened to reality,
Found himself feeding with the swine,
I, too, find myself
Dining on the husks of this world
Instead of banqueting at the King's table.
He could have stayed
Under the tender care of his father.
He chose, rather, to wander afar.
How like him am I, Lord.
Oftentimes wandering afar,
Dwelling midst strangers in an alien land,
Wasting the substance You have given,
Careless with my inheritance,
Seeking, searching, but unsatisfied.
Until . . . like the Prodigal,
I too am awakened by Thy Holy Spirit,
And like a crushed, snubbing child,
I run back to You, my Father,
Only to discover that You are still waiting,
With arms outstretched.
You place Your robe of righteousness about me.
Neither do You chide.
You only love me,
And tenderly take me in Your arms
Where You nourish and comfort me.
Thank You, Father,
That You still take the straying lambs in Your arms.
So I am renewed,
And my soul cries
"Abba . . . Father."

11.

Lord,
"This cup" You called it
That agonizing night in Gethsemane
When, knowing the terrible price You were to pay,
You pled with The Father three times
That it might pass from You,
While insensitive, drowzy disciples slept.
I cannot comprehend the awfulness of that moment
When You fully realized the penalty
You were to pay,
Not so much of death
(You were not afraid of that)
But of enduring the hiding of The Father's face
When in that hour You became sin.
The hideousness of "this cup"
Was that You, without sin, righteous,
Would actually become sin.
My sin . . . the world's sin.
No one ever drank such a bitter cup.
No dregs were ever so foul.
I do not wonder that You sweat drops of blood
As the awareness of what You were to become
Swept over Your human form.

I am grateful, Lord,
That in Your humanity,
You, like me, did not relish such a cup,
And asked The Father if there were any other way.
Not because You were afraid,
But because You were righteous, holy,
Without sin.
Such sorrow.
Such pain.

Such agony.
I rejoice today, My Lord and My God,
That You did not let the horror of that realization
Keep You from that rough-hewn, rugged cross.
The cross had to be anticlimactic
After Gethsemane.
Lord, help me . . . help me to have the sensitivity
To hold back my tongue,
To prevent my mouth
From ever uttering a word about "my cup."
I can never,
No one can ever know anything
About a "cup" that compares with Yours.
Such a bitter cup.
But what sweetness issued forth from the sacrifice
That cup required.
Thank You, Lord,
For the bitter cup You drank . . . to the dregs.

12.

Lord,
All Thy works shall praise Thy name.
In turn, they move my heart to praise and adoration.
It was especially so this morning.
It was the moment between dawn and sunrise.
Darkness had not fled
But was being chased into hiding
By the near-approaching sun.
The moisture of the night
Had turned into an icy mantle,
Lovingly embracing the earth in
Lacy-patterned, delicate silver.
The intricate patterns of ice on bare tree limbs
Silhouetted against the gray but reddening sky
Were as a thousand arms stretched heavenward in prayer,
And as if kneeling in worship.
Here and there white wisps of fog
Caressed the wintry landscape,
But with the first hint of sunrise
Began drifting gracefully and slowly upward
Like a thousand spiraling columns of incense.
Like the fog, my heart ascended toward Thee,
In a holy, hushed worship
Of praise, joy, and adoration.
The earth is Thy footstool, O Lord.
How beautiful are the works of Thy hands.
How tenderly they show me You
And make my heart cry
"Abba . . . Father."

13.

Lord,
Forgive my irreverence,
But knowing You
Is a lot like being on dope.
Not euphoric, but habitual.
As one fix for the addict
Is both the prelude and magnet leading to the next,
So, one moment in communion with You
Is both the fulfillment for that moment
And the creator of my need for another.
Just as the addict is never satisfied,
Almost always progressing from soft to hard drugs,
So the saint is always seeking the deeper things of God.
And, Lord, I'm sorry to say,
But as the addict's habit must be fed, or die,
So the soul must feed on faith,
Or discover the desire for You has waned and grown cold.
It seems, Lord,
That life with You is paradoxical.
You satisfy, yet create hunger in me.
You quench my thirst while making me thirstier.
Yet, even when hungering and thirsting,
I am satisfied.
I am at peace.
Father, forgive the analogy,
But help me ever to seek
Till rivers of living water o'erflow my being
And my soul feeds on Thee, the living bread.
So be it, Abba . . . Father,
Till I want no more.

14.

Lord,
It's happened twice this week.
One came by mail,
The other was left on my desk by an employee.
Both were expressions of thanks
For what, to me, were insignificant things
Which I never dreamed were causes for "thank you" notes.
They brought to me again a sharp awareness
That it is often the small, the little,
The unobtrusive things
That reach out in love to others
In the midst of a cold, uncaring world,
And touch their lives in a moment of tenderness.
I was not aware that I had done anything
Worthy of their notes of thanks.
But they had taken the time to let me know.
It shamed me in a way, Lord,
For how often have I been the recipient
Of kindness, of love, a gracious act
For which I have neglected to express
A word of thanks.
Thus, I have lost the chance
To share a sublime moment of eternity
With a fellow man.
My two friends may never know
The humility they brought to my heart
By their expressions of gratitude,
But for me, they came at a time
When I needed them.
In meeting their need (though unconsciously)
Love was put in motion which in turn met mine.
Love never goes unnoticed.

It has its own reward
Except when done to receive a reward.
Thank You, Lord,
For Your love, which is the source of all love,
And was essentially the fountain
From which my love . . . and theirs sprang.
Thank You for the tender touches
Expressed in two simple "thank you" notes.

15.

Lord,
There's a little of the judge in all of us,
In me,
Eager to point the finger
In scorn and accusation,
In condemnation of the fallen
And utter contempt of the failure.
Unlike the judge with a just verdict
Who finds no pleasure in his sentence,
We gleefully, with a sense of smugness,
Pass judgment,
Proud that we have not fallen so low.
I thank You, Lord,
That You do not treat me thus.
Yet I deserve Your condemnation,
Your pointed finger.
Your judgment would be just,
But You give mercy instead.
Guilty and unworthy (like all others)
I find and receive
Only grace and love.
Could my heart only pass to others
That love, that tenderness, that forgiveness,
Full, free, and unpatronizing!
Lord, rid me of my cloak of self-righteousness
Pulled rigidly and tightly about me.
Help me to love the defeated, the lonely, the helpless.
Free me from scorn,
From judgment,
From accusation,
And the pointed finger!

16.

Lord,
It was a nostalgic day.
A sad, happy, poignant day.
Yesterday I went back to the town of my childhood
Along with my brothers and sisters
To attend a funeral.
Relatives and friends not seen since boyhood
Gathered in the little town
Whose better days have long since vanished
And whose citizens are also at that place
Of swift successive trips to the cemetery.
It is now a town of old, dying people,
Living, if at all, on the memories of yesteryear.
But, Lord,
They were beautiful.
There was weather-beaten character etched
In faces of flint.
Time had eroded trenches in their skin
And courage in their hearts.
Their world is so uncomplicated, so simple,
Limited to a ten-mile radius, hard work, and few basic needs.

They remembered me, Lord.
They reminded me of childhood joys.
They hugged my neck
And said "Is this really Peaches?"
I hadn't been called that for many years.
They wouldn't even know my real name, Lord.
Surprisingly, I remembered them.
It was unbelievable that after so many years
I could remember people, now aged,
Whom I had last seen when they were young or middle-aged
And I was a child.

Thank You, Lord,
For the joy of going back to my childhood town.
Some things change, but it seems to be the same.
Drab, dreary, dead.
But dear . . . and friendly . . .
And home.

17.

Father,
Why is it we so easily get encumbered?
It seems to be our nature
That we become burdened
Under the weighty load of living,
Anxious, concerned, full of care.
Ambition plagues us,
Things possess us,
Either by their lack or possession,
And we carry all the days of our lives
Troubles and burdens You never meant us to bear.
The disgusting thing about it is that
They come to us so easily, so naturally.
And we cling to them, embrace them,
Clasp them to our bosoms
Like so many security blankets.
You told us, Lord,
To be anxious for nothing.
You also told us how to accomplish this miracle
When You said "in everything, by prayer and supplication,
With thanksgiving, let your requests be made known unto God,
And the peace of God, which passeth understanding,
Shall keep your hearts and minds . . ."
Oh, Father,
Keep my heart and mind.
Teach me to be so unencumbered
That when death comes,
The only thing left to give You
Will be this earthly body.

Lord,
I've thought of her all day.
It's her birthday, and I have been remembering
What a red-faced baby she was,
And what a surprise to her brothers and sister
Who just couldn't understand why they had to go to bed
So early the night she was born . . . at home.
And when she was just a baby
We wanted to die
When we thought she was going to . . . with polio.
She was a scrawny girl
And claims to this day
That I herded her around
By a firm grip on her neck.
In high school she was so beautiful.
Especially in that red crepe dress I bought her.
I was so thrilled I could take care of her
Through that last year in high school.
I felt fatherly the night she graduated.
But I felt so lonesome the night she got married
And I was seven hundred miles away.
She managed without me, and suddenly
She was a mother . . . once, twice, and a third time.
First thing I knew
She got farther and farther away,
Both in miles, and in her own new world.
Now, Lord, she's matronly.
My baby sister.
How dare she grow up
And make a middle-aged man of her brother?
Bless her, Lord,
For my baby sister turned forty today.

19.

Lord,
Lives of great men do remind us,
Probe us and prod us . . . even paralyze us.
For, though their lives have been sublime,
It does not necessarily follow that we can do likewise.
The fact is, Lord,
That trying to attain the heights
Others have attained,
Attempting to emulate, either in action or attitude,
The greatness of others
Can be a deadening experience.
We compare ourselves to others . . . a sure path
To self-condemnation.
There are always those more capable,
More attractive, more sophisticated,
More talented, lovelier, richer than we.
Then we don't like ourselves.
We immobilize our own abilities and capacities.
We neutralize our own potential into nothingness.
It is so easy, Lord,
To forget that You have designed me.
I am the only one in all the universe just like me.
No one else can be what I can be.
No one else can do what I can do.
Of all the billions of people on earth,
I am unique, by Your direction and creation.
It is wrong of me to expect me to be more than You expect.
It is wrong for me not to accept me as You accept me.
It is wrong for me to seek a way out of being me.
That does not mean, Lord,
That I am not to see the beauty in others,
To let their lofty lives inspire me to be

All that I can be,
To challenge me to let You make of my unique life
The highest life possible.
You have given us these examples
To encourage and inspire.
Give us the wisdom, Lord,
To be satisfied with that which You have made us . . .
Physically, emotionally, socially, intellectually,
So that we are not paralyzed by self-condemnation,
But inspired to reach the heights
Of Your purpose in our lives,
As, being ourselves, indwelt by Your Spirit,
We become all You meant us to become.

20.

Lord,
Your word tells us that everything has its season.
Even illness.
I've had a high fever all day, Lord.
My head is reeling with pain, and
Every bone aches, as I lie here
Horizontal and hurting.
But it has been such a good day.
It's been so quiet.
I've slept fitfully,
Read Your word and a number of books
While warm, soft music from the radio
Has played peacefully.
In this prone position and quietness
My heart has turned to You,
Both in my waking and sleeping moments.
You have been in this room,
Your all-pervading presence has been felt
And even in the fever and discomfort
I have leaned on You as my Comforter.
In addition, I've been babied and pampered
By the girls . . . by my wife.
Even the dog has known something is wrong
And looked sympathetically
With her sad, brown eyes.
I've wondered how the office could manage without me,
But it has, and very well, too!
Thank You, Lord,
For this quiet, sick day.

You even know when we need a day to be ill.
Truly, You are Wisdom.
You are the great designer of our days.
Thank You, Abba . . . Father.

21.

Abba . . . Father,
Thank You for the shallows of life!
In the shallow places I can stand upright
With a sure foundation under my feet.
In the shallows I feel a certain safety . . .
A safeguard, a security,
A preparation for the depths.
It is not evil to be shallow.
Every ocean has a shore.
Life is lived mostly in the shallows,
And they can be more treacherous than the deeps,
For when we live in the depths
We exert more caution.
The deep places come, Lord,
To give color and harmony
To the monotone of the shallows.
Father, teach me not to desire the depths
Out of spiritual pride
That others may see and know
How deep I am.
Help me not to fake the depths
Lest others come for a word of wisdom
Only to be left hopeless.
Rather, Lord, help me learn the lesson
Of faithfulness . . . in the shallows,
Lest I learn the truth in the depths
That I am the shallowest of all.

Lord,
She lavished her love upon You
And they indignantly accused her,
Saying her sacrifice was a waste.
How ignorant and unfeeling they were,
How wise and loving was she.
It was an alabaster box
Filled with a very costly fragrant ointment.
It was so expensive that its price
Would equal a year's pay
For any of the men who watched.
In an act of devotion and worship
She broke the box, pouring its precious contents
In one decisive motion
Upon Your head, Lord.
They murmured that it was only a waste,
That it should have been sold
And the money given to the poor.
Their blind and jealous hearts
Caused them not to see and understand
Her motive was love,
Her act was worship.
For You, Lord, commended her,
Reminding them, and us,
That she had anointed You for burial.
She had seen You were to die.
She understood with a wisdom divine
That You were to be the greatest sacrifice
Of which hers was incomparable, yet prophetic.
In understanding and perceiving
She did what she could,
Regardless of the cost.

You said, Lord, that wherever the gospel was preached
She would be remembered.
In remembering, I am helping fulfill that prophecy
Which, in itself, is simply one more proof
That You are the Son of God,
Worthy of her sacrifice of love,
And my praise.
Help me learn to lavish my love upon You
As simply, beautifully, and sacrificially as this woman.

Lord,
I'm making no promises today.
I know better.
The broken ones lie in heaps at my feet,
All painful reminders of good intentions
And earnest desires . . . unkept.
Thank You, Lord,
That I have learned
You are not an exactor of promises,
For You know our frame.
You remember we are dust,
Unable to keep that which we so honestly vow.
Youth's tender heart wept in frustration
At its inability to perform as promised.
Years of experience have taught
That tears cannot substitute
For the release to be found
In grace alone.
Free grace. Full grace. Undemanding grace.
Just because You love us.
No strings attached.
No conditional clauses.
No performance required.
No worthiness needed.
No works necessary.
Thank You, Lord, for the freedom
Both to do . . . and not to do.
And help me remember
You are the Promiser. . . .
I am the receiver!

Lord,
What is it with me anyway?
I don't see visions,
Or hear voices,
Or speak in any language other than my native tongue.
You don't perform miracles in my life.
You don't speak audibly to me,
Or lead me in strange, exotic paths,
Or cause me to do so many strange things
Like others I know claim You do for them.
What am I? A second-class Christian?
One lady I know, Lord,
Says she has a "hot line" direct to You.
Apparently she does.
But not me.
I yearn for the spectacular experience,
The mystic moments, the glorious visions.
I long for the "thrill."
Instead, I tread the plain path of sightless faith.
Ordinary and unexciting,
But the path You have chosen for me.
I really wouldn't trade places, Lord.
Though mine is unglamorous and unspectacular,
It is the path of communion with You,
A fellowship no experience could replace.
I do know peace that passes all understanding,
Joy unspeakable, blessed assurance,
And an unshaken confidence that You are all in all.
The Gracious Presence, the Good Shepherd,
My Friend, My Lord, My God.
I thank You for those who know more of You,

For those who experience more of the supernatural than I.
Maybe they have a greater need for it.
Thank You, Lord,
That for me, You are enough.

Lord,
I cannot possibly know how he felt.
I can only reach out to him
Father heart to father heart.
His beautiful daughter, a lovely college student,
Was in a grinding auto crash.
For weeks she lay unconscious.
The doctors gave little hope for recovery,
And the little hope they gave was tempered with the knowledge
That if she lived it might be in an impaired mental state.
The friends rallied to their side.
The church prayed.
The parents waited . . . and hoped.
Consciousness began to return very slowly.
She is still speechless, possibly forever.
Her beauty is marred, but life has been spared.
Her father spoke last week in church,
To thank the folk and to inform them of her progress.
He said "this incident was no accident."
He spoke of faith, hopes, dreams.
And all the while he spoke, Lord,
I was putting myself in his place.
I too have a lovely teen-aged daughter
For whom I have great love and aspirations.
Yet I still have my daughter, fresh, beautiful, and healthy.
Were mine like his, how would I feel, Lord?
Would I speak of faith, or would I be bitter?
Would I exude hope, or hopelessness?
I hurt for him! I wanted to say "I understand"
But I knew I didn't. What could I know?
Only love.
The father heart in me reached out to the father heart in him,

Though he never knew it,
And I ached, and wept inwardly,
And prayed fervently.
"Like as a father pitieth his children."
Bless that dear man, Lord!
I pray that Your Father love will reach out to comfort.
Not just that father, but all who have been touched by her life.
The daughter may actually have the easier part.
She is not suffering the pain of a broken daughter.
Thank You, Lord,
For my dear daughter.
I pray that I may never have a burden like his to bear.
But . . . if I do, help me, Lord,
To bear it in faith and confidence,
Like the example of this father.
Bring glory and good out of "this incident . . . no accident."

Lord,
A leper once came to You and said,
"If You are willing You can make me clean."
And You were willing.
A woman touched the hem of Your garment,
And You were willing.
A little, short Zacchaeus needed a friend,
And You were willing.
Mary Magdalene, who had seven demons,
Lazarus, who was dead,
Peter, who denied,
John, who loved.
All these were needy,
Each in a different way
And You were willing.
Thank You, Father,
That for a hungry heart, a longing soul
You are always willing.
Thank You that for me
You were willing
And took me, just as I was,
Never demanding worthiness . . . only need.
Teach me, Lord,
To be willing to reach out
To touch those who need You,
To help them learn that all their need
Can be met by You.
Now I understand a little more
Of what You meant when You said
"Lo, I come to do thy will. . . ."
Thank You, Lord,
That for this day, this hour,
You are still willing.

27.

Father,
We had a wonderful celebration today.
A joyful celebration.
Some would call it a funeral,
But not my friend,
Not Margaret, whose body we placed in the earth today.
It was *coronation day* for her,
For she met her King, face to face.
She heard Him say, "Welcome home, child."
So, we celebrated.
We were joyous . . . for her sake.
It was not that she was homesick.
She would have liked to stay longer,
But she was ready,
And she loved You so deeply.
She knew whatever You wanted was best.
She also loved life, and lived it zestfully,
As a missionary in Spain, in Cuba,
As a preacher's wife,
As my first employee.
It seems she was so young to go,
But she had lived well.
There were no regrets.
The cancer was quick,
And practically painless.
Bless her husband, Lord.
He will feel the loss so keenly.
He knows You well enough
That there will be no bitterness . . . only joy
That she is now eternally joyful.
Thank You, Lord, for Margaret.

41

A devoted wife, a faithful employee,
A good friend, a precious saint.
If I were You,
I would want her "home" too!

Lord,
The prophets of doom are at it again.
Raving . . . raging . . . fiery . . . ferocious
In their vehement prophesying.
I've heard it so many times.
It seems the prophets are almost glad
To make their dire predictions.
They do it with such gusto, and such vengeance.
Yet, Lord,
Why is there the gnawing fear deep inside me
That this time they may be right?
Oh, not all of them.
Some are blatant opportunists; some are showmen.
But some are good men, honest men
With the firm conviction
They are spokesmen to warn this generation.
Those are the ones who trouble me.

Did it bother John the Baptist
When he called his contemporaries a "generation of vipers"?
Poor Jeremiah was so upset by his own prophecies
He wept buckets of tears.
I know Isaiah spoke with a broken heart.
Yet the people of their day
Felt towards prophets much as I do, Lord,
That most of them are a crazy lot
Not worth my time.
Yet . . . yet . . .
There is so much truth to their pronouncements.
There does seem to be justification
For their accusations
That we have gone too far this time.

I just don't know, Lord.
Prophets never have been a very popular people.
Nor have their warnings been heeded.
Nobody believed Noah
Until it was too late.
Lord, teach us not to panic
When the fire and brimstone words spew forth,
But help us to have wisdom enough to discern
Between the false and true,
And act accordingly.
How good to know, Lord,
That when the judgments fall
The judge of all the earth will do right.
What great assurance to believe that even in judgment
You are behind it all, controlling, directing
To that end which You know is good and right.
Thank You, Lord,
For faith in the face of wrath.

29.

Father,
Drifting comes so easily.
Aimlessness sneaks its way into my life,
Cheating and defrauding me of the best.
Suddenly, the remainder of the journey
Is so much shorter than that already traveled,
And it is so much later than I had dreamed.
I discover I have not learned
To number my days
Nor apply my heart unto wisdom.
All because it is easier to be carefree and gay
Than determined and intent.
It seems now that there has been
Much motion but little direction.
Maybe, Lord,
It is just that today is New Year's
And I've been taking stock.
It's not that I'm unsuccessful or unhappy,
But a new year, like each successive birthday,
Has a ruthless way of revealing the truth
That I have not attained all my goals,
Or even done my best.
Lord, help me not to be too hard on myself,
Neither let me permit myself to get by
With substituting the good for the best.
Father, keep me from the silent but deadly enemy
Of drifting.
Teach me, Lord,
To have both motion and direction
And apply my heart unto wisdom.
It is later than I thought.

30.

Lord,
I thank You for all the trophies of grace
You have brought to Yourself.
I thank You that You died for sinners,
The ungodly, the unrighteous, like me.
But Lord, I'm just a mite fed up
With "trophy" Christians.
Showcase Christians who (perhaps through no fault of their own)
Are put on display before us as shining examples
Like "before" and "after" ads.
Drug addicts, pushers, pimps,
Stripteasers, prostitutes, gangsters,
Wrestlers, football stars, beauty queens.
The parade is almost endless.
At the drop of a Bible they are eager
To detail explicitly their lives "before"
For all the world to hear . . . and the young to envy.
It almost strikes fear into my heart
To see the saints, fascinated, spellbound,
Hanging on to every word,
Savoring vicariously all the thrills
They dare not experience personally.
Lord, I'm not upset with the "trophies" . . . it isn't their fault.
I am disturbed that we parade these people
And glamourize their lives in such a way
That the young people feel they must emulate the "before"
Instead of the "after."
We leave the impression that without the depths of sin
We cannot know the riches of Your grace.
Lord, I cannot believe You put a premium upon those
Whose past lives have been lived in degradation
Any more than those whose lives have been more respectable.

The thing that seems to escape most is that
You love sinners.
So, You love us all.
We are all sinners.
The degraded as well as the respectable.
Deep sin is no worse than respectable sin.
Teach us, Lord,
Not to encourage the uninitiated
To a life of gross sin by our overglamourization of it.
And help the "trophies" who have been put in the limelight
That it may not lead to pride, or their downfall
When the glamour is gone.

31.

Lord,
My pulse beats faster,
My stomach churns,
And all the old resentment returns
Whenever I see him,
Or read about his success,
Or let my mind dwell upon him.
I don't like to be this way, Lord.
I don't want these feelings, but I seem helpless.
He was my best friend.
We were coworkers for many years
And I loved him.
I guess I still do or I wouldn't hurt so badly.
I know now it was not all his fault.
But I only learned mine after it was all over.
He knew what he was doing from the first.
When the break came I felt betrayed, deserted,
And worse, that he had used me, Lord,
For his own end, only to discard me as useless
When his purpose had been served.
The hardest part, Lord, was having to watch
As through the succeeding years
You have used him far and wide,
Made him famous,
And glorified Yourself through his ministry.
All the while my heart has wept,
Wondering at how You could use him!
Until You helped me understand.
You, Lord, are sovereign, and You are just.
You use whom You please, because You please,
And You are not obligated to explain to anyone.
You used a rooster to convict Peter,

An ass to speak to Balaam.
It is Your business, not mine.
I thank You, Lord, for using him.
I have learned a priceless lesson.
Now, Lord, mature me sufficiently that I do not hurt,
Nor begrudge his success,
But from my heart of hearts
Can love him, and pray for him,
Wishing for him all I would wish for myself.
Teach me to trust You,
Knowing that what You choose to do with another
Is none of my business.

32.

Lord,
Change is, at best, a painful process.
It takes a whole lifetime.
In my haste, I want it to happen yesterday.
I am so impatient to be what I envision in the future.
So, blunderingly, I aim for that central spot on the horizon
That epitomizes complete change,
Only to discover, when that point is reached
The goal itself has changed.
Life is one whole change
From mortal to immortal,
And the process of steady change
That takes place between these two points
Is the color of and the challenge to life itself.
Part of me longs for change
While the other fights for its very life
Against those changes,
Fearful of the new and untried or unfamiliar.
I pray, Lord, that You will teach me
To be patient with myself,
Even more so than with others,
Neither fearful of nor rushing into change
For the variety it offers.
I pray for the grace of wisdom,
For the gift of discernment
That I may not unwisely resist change,
Nor impetuously rush headlong into it.
Help me, Lord, to be neither too quick
Nor too hesitant,
Conscious that change must come,
But never changing just for the novelty of it.
Do not let me be so foolish as to think

A change will correct all my circumstances
Or my attitudes.
Change me, Lord, into Your likeness,
Which, when reflected to others,
Will also change them.

33.

Lord,
Like Peter, and the rest of the human race
My heart often asks,
"What's in it for me, Lord?"
A natural question
But an unworthy one.
The answer is almost irrelevant, Lord,
For whatever it may be, I am unalterably committed,
Having gone beyond the point of no return,
Unable, unwilling, not desiring to turn back.
For were there nothing in it for me,
This life with You, Lord,
Is far better than any other available to man,
And would be in itself enough reward.
When life with You, Lord, is known in reality,
Any other pales into nothingness in comparison.
Whatever any other life style offers,
It cannot offer hope, peace, or joy.
It cannot offer unselfish
Or sacrificial love.
None other can give the power to cope
With *life,* in all its drabness, its tawdriness,
With the assurance that everything is as it should be
And one day it will all be understood
As being allowed by You,
And as being good.

But, Lord,
You did give an answer to the question.
You promised a hundredfold in this life in return,
And eternal life hereafter.
I am not naïve enough, Lord,

To believe that any materialistic or commercial gain
Is the direct reward You give in return for faithfulness.
If so, that would be a bribe.
No . . . It is far deeper than that.
It *is* a hundredfold in return.
There are hundreds of homes
Where I am welcome, to eat or sleep.
There are hundreds of brothers and sisters
I count as mine.
The returns are more than hundredfold,
They are countless.
Oh, the treasures You give, Lord,
Are so much richer than the treasures of this earth.
You also promised eternal life.
I have it . . . Now . . . not someday.
Thank You, Lord.
Thank You for all there *is* in it for me.

꧁ ꧂

Abba . . . Father!
The wonder of it all.
You made me and fashioned (designed) me in Your image.
You never created an imperfection.
So . . . everything in me that is not like You
Is alien, foreign . . . an intruder . . . a perversion,
Without a right to be there.
If You fashioned, designed me,
It was not only to Your specifications
But according to Your will
And for my good.
Thus, Father,
All that I am,
All that I like or dislike,
All that I feel is good, or bad,
Is from Your hand
Intended for me,
Designed for me,
Directed to me
To conform me to Your image.
If this is so, to complain about what I am
Is rebellion, unmitigated and raw,
Against You, Lord.
What sweet relief and release
To know that I am what I am
By Your creation and design.
I need never again struggle against me,
Or chafe at what You have made me.
I need only rest in Your work,
Knowing that I see darkly
While You see perfection.

Lord,
Forgive my foolish, insipid,
My ignorant, terribly immature praying.
I ask You to be with me
When You have said already, "Lo, I am with you always . . ."
I ask You to go with me
When You have said, "I will never leave thee . . ."
I ask You to give me strength,
To fill me with love,
To help me be what You want me to be.
Very worthy ideals, but not possible.
This is not Your way.
Lord, I've prayed so earnestly
And tried so hard to be what You want
Only to discover
You are not interested in helping me,
Or giving me strength,
Or guiding, or filling me.
So late I've discovered
You do not want to help.
Rather, You want to be all I need.
You will not give me strength,
You give me Yourself . . . strength.
You do not give direction;
You are the Guide.
You do not go with me;
You *are* with me.
Your plan is that I find in You
My sufficiency, my adequacy,
My all in all.
If You granted strength,
I would miss the blessing of finding

You are my strength.
Thank You, Father,
That You do not answer all my silly, stupid prayers.
Teach me to learn
I have no lack or need
Which is not, or cannot be, met in You,
My Lord and my God.

Lord,
The hardest part of all
Is keeping a simplicity in life.
And especially, the simplicity of the gospel.
How easily we get sidetracked, almost imperceptibly,
Until awakened to the sudden realization
That the simplicity is gone,
Replaced by complexity, systems, and regulations
Binding us inextricably in a morass of
"Thou shalt" and "Thou shalt not."
Everything has become so difficult,
So complicated, Lord.
No wonder the young are going back to nature,
To the communes, to the basics in life.
I do not want their life style, except for its simplicity.
The most discouraging part of all
Is that the gospel has become so intricate.
We live in a maze of meetings and standards
You did not set, Lord.
We gauge the quality of a person's spirituality
By the number of times they attend church,
Or the many offices they hold,
Or the rules they keep.
St. Paul warned the Corinthians
That to depart from the simplicity to be found in Christ
Was to be beguiled by the serpent.
How we have been tricked, Lord,
How we have been deceived,
Oftentimes by the ministers of the gospel
Who have mistaken service for sanctification,
Complexity for quality, busyness for spirituality.
So much so, Lord,

That those who try to remain childlike and simple
In their relation to You
Are accused of either being lazy,
Indifferent, backslidden, or heretical.
Teach us, Lord, and help us
To get back to the basics
Of a personal relationship and fellowship with You,
Apart from which,
All other activities, rules, and regulations
Are a prostitution of the gospel.
Lord, lead us back to the simplicity of the gospel.

37.

Lord,
What a wild, unpredictable, glorious day this has been.
In spite of the fact that nothing which I planned was accomplished.
It was a great day.
We took the panel truck deep into the pine forests
To load firewood for the fireplace.
My youngest girl went along just to ride with Papa.
We sang as we drove the farm roads.
The deep blue lakes shimmered brightly
In the soft glow of a south winter sun.
We watched the cows grazing lazily,
Envying their pastoral quietness.
Then the van got stuck in a mud puddle.
We tried for an hour to get out—unsuccessfully.
Finally we went for help,
And their pickup got stuck.
At dark we got unstuck,
Just in time to gather about thirty logs.
But we laughed through it all.
We talked back to the cows
While they eyed us suspiciously.
Everything went wrong.
We got stuck. We got very little wood.
But we got so much we had not expected.
She held my hand, we sang, we laughed, we ran,
And loved each other the whole day.
She slept all the way home.
Once, when I sneezed, she asked, "What did you say, Papa?"
It was a fun-love day, Lord.
Thank You . . . and . . . do it again, Lord.

38

Lord,
They just left.
Silence fills every room.
The house is still and quiet
Where yesterday the happy hubbub
Of a family reunion was taking place.
It was the first in six years.
For the first time
There were no new nieces or nephews.
Those who were just children the last time
Were now practically grown.
The boys had their cars,
The girls their boyfriends.
The mamas and papas were looking more than ever
Like a bunch of expectant grandparents.
One couple had already reached that heady status.
Sickeningly so.
No one ever had grandchildren before.
What a happy time we had.
Incessant chatter, giggles, laughter.
There was too much food
And not enough of each other.
We didn't even have a family fuss.
One was missing from the family
Since our last time together.
The pain of it was evident at times.
For one we had an early birthday party
With presents and a cake.
She first thought it was an anniversary cake
For one of the couples.
When she realized it was for her, she cried.
She is the mother . . . the aging grandmother.

We may not have her the next time
And we realized it silently. No one dared verbalize it.
The memories moved among us all the day.
Age and youth, and those in between,
Mingled in a joyous, raucous bedlam for twenty-four hours.
What a short time for families to be together.
And now they are gone.
The sweet sadness remains.
The poignancy lingers.
Who will not be among us next time?
What heartaches and joys will have invaded these lives
Before we are together again?
Thank You, Lord, for the family.
Bless each of them . . . their children . . . their grandchildren.
Thank You for that larger family
Of which You are the Head,
And for the joy of knowing that one day
There will never be separation again.
Thank You, Lord,
For our family reunion.

39.

Lord,
You said "Come unto me . . . and I will give you rest."
Thank You for the rest I have found in You.
Rest from ceaseless striving,
From wearying anxieties,
From selfish struggle.
There can be no rest
Where there is no firm foundation.
So, in You, I can cast my whole weight
In utter abandon and complete confidence,
For You are my rock upon which I stand,
Firmly grounded by faith
In the eternal verities of the Word.
Lord, it took so long to find rest,
Even after coming to You.
It would not have been meaningful
Had it come quickly, automatically,
Without a struggle.
Now I have proved to my own heart
That all else is vain,
All else is hopeless and futile,
And apart from total, holy obedience and abandon,
Rest is impossible.
Like the raging sea,
Mankind churns in unrest,
Looking, searching, longing, seeking
To no avail.
Lord, help me to hold forth
The ministry of peace,
The message of rest.
Our world is so weary,
So hopeless, so angry.

Raise up shepherds who can lead to green pastures,
To still waters,
To quiet, serene, unperturbed rest
Found only in You, the Great Shepherd of my soul.

40

Lord,
I see and feel the shadows today.
My world is full of gray,
A dull, colorless monotone.
I cannot pinpoint the cause,
But I know with force the effect.
It is not depression or despondency,
Just sort of a shadowy nether-world gray.
A blah.
A powerlessness. A helplessness.
I am not desperate,
Nor do I feel panic.
It is more an un-feeling,
An unattachment, a waiting.
Thank You, Lord, for these infrequent days.
The shadows must come.
Days of gray are reminders that
Life is not always a bright hued palette
Of sunshine and roses,
Of rainbow and laughter,
Of pink-cloud radiance.
These are the days that remind me
That I have this human treasure in an earthen vessel.
I am clay.
I am vulnerable.
I am dependent.
I am weak.
But . . . I am Yours.
And that makes a gray day
Fit into the pattern of a full life,
Just as threads into a beautiful fabric.
Lord, I long for the growth and maturity

That makes me sing
When the shadows are long,
When the heart is heavy,
When the burdens are wearying.
Grant me the wisdom to know
That every day is a gift from You,
Designed and directed to me
To make a life full and rich,
A life that has tasted of joy and sorrow,
Pain and pleasure,
Defeat and victory,
Gray and rainbows.
Thank You, Lord,
For this waiting day . . . this growing day.
This gray day . . . the prelude to tomorrow.

41.

Lord,
Thank You that You did not look for big things to do.
You were not afraid of the commonplace . . . the routine.
Like the time You took a towel
And began to wash the disciples' feet.
I do not believe that was a pleasant task,
But You did it,
For it simply needed to be done,
And we needed the example.
Their feet were rough and dirty,
And they must have smelled badly.
Surely there was no thrill in it for You,
Except the thrill of serving another's need.
I doubt there was any great illumination
Or mystic call to such a task.
Rather, Lord, it was common, dull,
Perhaps even drudgery.
Yet in such a lowly and mean task
You exhibited the marvel of grace.
You were not hindered from the job before You
Because it was unglamorous, or big,
Or breathtakingly exciting.
It was plain, everyday, and menial
Yet it had to be done, and You did it.
Lord, how I need to learn to take a towel
And wash the feet . . . or hands . . . or head of others,
Or give a cup of cold water,
Or a bowl of hot soup to a sick neighbor,
Or play a game of dominoes with an aged saint,
Or checkers with a child.
Lord, help me learn
That each task I do, whether small or large,

When it is done as unto You,
Is endued with a holiness
Unmatched by all the world's exciting tasks.
Lord, help me learn
To take a towel.

42.

Lord,
My teen-ager and I both learned a good lesson today.
We were going to re-do her room.
New carpet, new paint, new bedspread and curtains.
The works.
And, because she was getting to the place
Where she was ready to assert independence,
She insisted on picking the color of the paint.
Yellow.
Bright, orange, garish yellow.
Loud, screaming yellow.
But it was her decision,
And we relented to her wishes.
Her mother painted the walls
While she was in school.
I had to close the door when I saw it,
For it made me sick to my stomach.
I had so hoped it would turn out to be
A dainty, feminine, sunshine-crisp
But soft yellow.
Like a daffodil, a daisy, or a girl.
When she got home from school
She rushed to her room.
The look on her face was evidence
She, too, was disappointed.
But, because she had insisted,
She faked delight, and
Held tightly to her claim that this was the color she wanted.
The evening crept on into night.
She slept in another room.
The next morning she bravely admitted
She had made a mistake.

That we were right.
And that she should have listened to her parents.
Lord,
Thank You for my mature young lady.
It was bound to be hard for her.
We would have let her keep her color,
But she knew in her heart she couldn't live with it.
So, lovingly, she asked if we would mind
If we painted it a softer yellow.
Which we gladly did.
She learned the lesson that
It is good to admit mistakes,
And that parents can sometimes be right.
And we learned that even in independence
Children still need the wiser guidance
Of more mature years in some things,
Even if it has to go against the wishes of the younger.
Bless my teen-ager, Lord,
And may her room be a sweet sanctuary
For her maturing years.

43.

Lord,
Thank You for the sandpapers of life.
The things that grate, that rub,
That irritate.
It's not that I like them.
I need them.
It is my reaction to the sandpapers
That counts.
It is here You show me what I am.
I find from the sandpapers
That I am rough and raw
And I need smoothing.
The rubbing hurts, Lord,
And the pain of the repeated friction
Is at times almost unbearable.
The hurt is even more,
Realizing that what I thought had already become smooth
Is such a jagged mountain.
Why is it, Lord,
I seem never to learn
Except when it hurts?
Thank You, Lord,
For every wound rubbed raw
By the sandpapers of life.
And, Lord,
Keep smoothing me . . . keep smoothing me
Until I am conformed
To Your image.

44.

Lord,
I *have* been considering the lilies of the field,
Just like You said I should.
They don't toil. . . .
They don't spin. . . .
They are gloriously clothed.
Effortlessly radiant,
Quietly serene,
They bob about as mute reminders
Of a way of life You mean me to know.
I toil. . . . I spin. . . .
Oh, how I spin.
And with far less results.
I love the lilies, Lord.
You do wonderfully care for them.
You do give them a stunning beauty.
Yet they are here today, gone tomorrow.
I know my life is far more important to You than theirs,
For You said so.
Yet I do not know how to be careless,
Trusting, abiding, yielding as the lilies.
I take thought about tomorrow.
I am concerned about how I will be clothed.
So do the pagan, heathen peoples
Who know no God.
You know me, Lord.
You know my needs.
Your love for me is far beyond
Your love for the lilies.
Your care for me far exceeds
Any earthly flower, shrub, or tree.
Your Word says You will give me all that I need

71

If I but seek You first.
And the birds of the air . . .
I saw a cardinal this morning, Lord.
Regal, crimson, stately, and beautiful.
He never knew I saw him, for he was eating.
Freely partaking of the abundance of Your bounteous provision.
He had not sown the seed,
Or tended the garden,
Or sweated because of the labor of his brow.
He simply partook . . . because You provided.
I know I am more important than a cardinal,
Or a sparrow, or robin, or eagle,
For You told me so.
But I work, I worry,
I store up food . . . and fuss about the prices.
Lord, how lovely are the lilies,
How beautiful the birds of the air.
Teach me to trust, to cast aside anxiety,
To look to You . . . for I am the peculiar object of Your love.
Thank You, Lord, for the lesson of
The lilies and the birds.

45

Lord,
I thank You for the many hoaryheaded saints
Whose lives have quietly, but firmly,
Blazed a glorious path before me,
And who still stand as shining examples of faith
To the many witnesses who have watched . . . and wondered.
Thank You for Ellen, who, at seventy-three
Could still turn cartwheels and hearts,
To whom life was always an adventure,
And for whom my eldest is named.
Thank You for J.P., the father of twenty churches
In one city alone.
At ninety-five, still stalwart and steady,
A constant reminder to all of the wisdom and grace You impart
To a life wholly given to You.
Thank You for Mama B., an aged saint
Given to a life of prayer for anyone in need.
Her prayers always seemed to have a direct line to You.
Thank You for Mimie, a frail housewife . . . childless . . .
Who had countless children in the Lord
And whose life resulted in hundreds of preachers,
Teachers, missionaries, and lay people.
Thank You for Dr. Mac.
Resolute, sturdy, pioneer stock, oil man,
Wealthy, firm (some would say crude),
Eloquent pulpiteer, gentle-hearted,
With a great love for children and young preachers.
Thank You for Cassie . . .
Beloved colored saint, church janitor, heavenly soul.
Dignity personified, he rode his white stallion through town
Each morning on his way to work.
Lord, I do love the dear old saints.

Thank You for their wisdom, their gentility, their nobility,
Their sturdiness to face life
With both godliness and contentment.
They have prayed for me in my immaturity.
They have loved me for Your sake.
They have seen what lies underneath
And overlooked what they have seen.
Their faith has been unwavering and unquenchable.
I pray for each of these today,
And for all older saints.
Help them not to feel neglected or unloved.
May the joy they have given others
Return a hundredfold to them.
Help me to bring forth fruit in my old age,
As these have done.

46.

Lord,
The last box has been loaded onto the moving van.
The empty house has been swept clean.
It stands bare, every nook exposed and nude,
Like a tree in the dead of winter.
Somehow the pain of leaving seems its worst just now.
Thank You, Lord, for the years spent here.
We all feel as if we're leaving a dear, close friend,
A part of the family,
And the pain of it grabs the insides.
So, in tribute to these walls that have sheltered us,
To these floors that have upheld us,
We gather in the master bedroom,
Sit on the floor, hold hands, and sing
"Alleluia, alleluia, alleluia, alleluia."
We can't look each other in the eye,
Knowing one look would suffice
To bring the dammed-up tears to overflowing.
So we sing, then pray, and leave
Our little red brick house-home-haven.
Thank You, Lord,
For a place to lay our heads, shuck our shoes,
A place in which we can love, or fuss,
Sing or pray,
Knowing that every experience of life within these walls
Has made it home.
Help us, Lord,
To learn from this experience,
That we should never take a house for granted.
May those who next abide within its sheltering walls
Know the joy we have known in this little home.

47

Lord,
Thank You that it is never too late.
Thank You there is no way to get beyond Your love.
I've thought many times I had gone too far,
That I had exhausted Your patience and love.
How little I knew of the infinite boundaries
Of Your care and tenderness.
As a shepherd with the bleeding lamb in his arms,
You have always brought me back.
As a Father pitying His child,
You have restored my soul.
Peter once felt hopeless and ashamed
After the crisis was over.
With typical bravado, he said,
"I'm going fishing."
What was there left to do, Lord?
His dream was shattered.
He had followed what appeared to be
A discredited impostor.
And now that the dream was dead
He did the only thing left to him . . . he went fishing.
Numbed, hopeless, crushed . . . he went fishing.
And caught nothing.
All night he and the others fished . . . for nought.
But, knowing how much Peter needed You,
You called to him from the shore.
At Your word they placed the nets
On the other side of the boat and caught so many fish
They could not haul in the net.
It was then they realized it was You,
And Peter, the streaker, put on his clothes,
Jumped in the water and came to You.

"Do you love me, Peter?"
"Yes, Lord."
"Feed my lambs."
Three times You asked;
Three times he answered,
Remembering with shame that he had denied You three times.
But that was now all erased,
Forever forgotten by You, Lord.
And Peter learned it is never too late.
For then You said, as You had done years before,
"Follow me."
And Peter knew there was no way to go
Beyond the reaches of Your love.
He knew . . . with certainty
It is never too late.

48.

Lord,
It is beyond the realm of my understanding.
You became a human being
In order to understand what I must endure
In temptation, in distress, in troubles,
And in joys.
Because of Your incarnation in human flesh,
The Word says You are touched by my infirmities.
"Touched."
Touched, Lord?
"Tempted."
Tempted, Lord?
In all points? Just like me?
Did You really endure all that being human means?
I remember You wept over Lazarus.
I recall Your love for Mary, Martha,
And especially for John, the beloved disciple.
You were angry with the money changers.
You even sweat drops of blood
And asked Your Father to let the cup
Which was Yours to drink to the bitter dregs
Pass from You, if possible.
I can understand those emotions.
But, Lord, I cannot quite grasp
That You were tempted, and thus touched by my need.
Like when I am jealous, or envious, materialistic,
Bitter, resentful, or lustful.
I cannot imagine You being capable of these things.
Yet, Your Word says You were tempted in *every* point . . . like me.
That means then that You really are touched
When I lust, or fear, or manipulate and scheme.
You understand and sympathize.

But oh, the difference.
For You never yielded
To those pulls of the flesh.
You never sinned.
If You really were human indeed,
How You must have suffered
When such temptations and desires
Came in upon You like a flood, as they do me.
Because of Your being God,
It must have grieved You so.
Because of Your having been human,
You now are touched by my needs, my infirmities.
It is a mystery beyond my comprehension,
But my heart bows in worship
To know that when I suffer with sin
You, too, are suffering with me,
Touched by my humanity.
Thank You, Lord,
For being "touched."

49.

Abba . . . Father!
You have told me in Your word
That it is good for me to draw near to You.*
You also have said if I draw near to You,
You will draw near to me.†
My heart yearns and cries out for such a nearness, Lord.
But like a sheep, I go astray,
Turning more often to my own way than to You.
It is then I groan in travail
For that release from this body into that liberty
For which all creation groans . . .
That liberty from the sinful nature
To which this body is entombed.
A liberty so full and free
It could only be contained in a new, glorious body
Which You have promised I will have one day.
Until then, teach me, Lord,
Lead me, Father,
To draw near to you,
Not only with my lips but with my heart,
For my spirit longs for Thee.
My soul thirsts after Thee.
My heart cries out for Thee.
So, I draw near
And await Your drawing near to me.
I come in penitence, in humility,
In gratitude, in love.
It is good to draw near to You.
Thank You, Abba . . . Father, for drawing near to me.

* Psalms 73:28
† James 4:8

50

Father,
I watched the tear roll down one side of her face,
And I ached to take her in my arms.
To comfort, solace, caress, and wipe away the tear,
Just as I had done so many times before.
But, Lord, I couldn't.
For some unjust reason,
Fathers feel clumsy when their daughters are fifteen.
The privileges change; the freedom is gone.
So, I wept inwardly for her
And could only mutter some foolish remark
Which held little or no comfort
As I remained awkwardly still.
Her problem was not very big, Lord,
Except to her. The hurt was big.
I knew she had been having it rough.
A new town . . . new school.
And even with her gregarious personality
There were still no real friendships.
She had been trying to ignore it,
To put up a front that all was well.
Discouragement and loneliness finally prevailed
And the salty tear fell silently and slowly.
Bless my dear teen-ager tonight, Lord.
Save her from self-pity.
Put the bounce back in her voice and in her step.
Restore the sweet smile and the tender heart.
She loves You, Lord,
And if a human could be worthy of Your blessing,
She is.

If she were a few years younger,
I could handle it myself.
But when a girl is fifteen, fathers must stand aside
And watch . . . and pray . . . and hurt inside.

51

Lord,
I bring my golden calves to You, today.
Not an actual golden facsimile idol,
But all my golden calf idols
At whose shrines I worship.
The children of Israel at least
Had a flimsy reason for their behaviour.
Moses had left them leaderless
To go atop a volcanic smoking mountain,
And they thought they had been deserted by both him
And God.
I don't even have their excuse, Lord.
To many they may not seem like golden calves,
But idols they are,
Whether golden calf
Or some other banal figure, figment, or fancy
To which we attach ourselves
With a devastating ferocity
Unworthy of great idols,
Much less of trivial ones.
The children of Israel were, at least,
Wholehearted in their veneration,
Shedding their clothes
For a frenzied, nude orgy . . .
All in the name of worship.
Thank You, Father,
That my golden calves are respectable.
Not wild nor wicked like the Israelites'.
Just plain middle-class, respectable idols.
They seem so harmless, so innocent,
Yet idols they are . . . devastating,
Demanding allegiance, decrying any damage.

So, Lord,
I bring You my golden idols.
Those I cannot destroy, I give to You
And they are now Your responsibility.
Those with a lesser hold, but still enjoyable,
I bring to You,
Asking You to make them unpleasant.
May my heart know no shrine
But Yours, Lord,
With no idol between to alienate.

52.

Lord,
My joints need oiling, my bones ache,
My back won't straighten up, and my hands are blistered.
It's spring-gardening time again.
All week long I have been working the soil,
Turning, weeding, spading, shoveling, raking.
I have stooped over so long at times
I can hardly stand upright again.
The sweat has run profusely down my face,
And finally, exhausted from good, hard physical labor,
A hot shower and a glass of iced tea refresh me.
Then I remember how good my body feels after hard work.
And rest . . . my sleep has been deep and restful.
Thank You, Lord,
For the joy of working in my garden.
I have not done any planting yet . . . just preparing the soil.
The tearing up and rooting out must come first.
How like me, Lord.
My life is constantly being torn up by You.
You dig ground . . . deep ground in me.
You root out the clay of hardness.
You pull out the weeds of neglect.
You turn the soil of unconcern and idleness.
You prepare me.
Will I ever be ready?
Will I ever be able to bring forth a harvest?
Will I ever be a productive ground
For Your work? For Your glory?
Lord, I ask You to be ruthless.
Spare nothing in me, as I spare nothing in my garden,
That would hinder growth and harvest.

Don't listen, Lord, when I cry "stop."
I don't mean it. At least I don't want to mean it.
Plow, turn, rake, spade, shovel, crush, root out,
Plant, water, feed . . . and harvest.

53.

Lord,
It was a holy moment, awesome,
Reverent, deep, and movingly tender.
He was ninety-five years old, hoaryheaded,
Full of life and love
And radiantly godly.
His nineteen-year-old daughter had been killed
Just the week before in an auto accident.
It was Wednesday night at the church.
He stood straight, though not very tall,
And asked permission to sing a song
That expressed his feelings.
He then began to sing in a firm, strong, but aged voice,
"Ask ye what great thing I know that delights and stirs me so?
What the high reward I win, Whose the name I glory in?
Jesus Christ, the Crucified.
What is faith's foundation strong, what awakes my lips to song?
He who bore my sinful load, purchased for me peace with God,
Jesus Christ, the Crucified."

Each verse was sung without accompaniment
And by memory.

"Who is life in life to me, Who the death of death will be?
Who will place me on His right with the countless hosts of light?
Jesus Christ, the Crucified.
This is that great thing I know; This delights and stirs me so:
Faith in Him Who died to save, Him Who triumphed o'er the grave,
Jesus Christ, the Crucified."*

The saints wept.
The angels rejoiced.

* "Ask Ye What Great Thing I Know"

87

My heart nearly burst.
Thank You, Lord, for that feeble saint
Who, through long years, had come to know
The Crucified.

54

Father,
Your words are hard.
Your disciples said so,
Not understanding many times what You meant.
I think, Lord, had I been there that day
I, too, would have said Your sayings were hard.
"Drink my blood. . . ."
"Eat my flesh. . . ."
"My blood is the true drink. . . ."
"My flesh is the true bread. . . ."
Hideous.
Revolting.
Nauseating.
At least it would have been to me.
It was to Your disciples,
And many of them turned away that day,
Never to follow You again.
You then turned to the inner circle and asked,
"Will You also go away?"
To which blustering Peter answered divinely,
"To whom shall we go, Lord?
You have the words of eternal life."
Oh, Father,
How many times, in utter desperation,
My heart has echoed Peter's sublime words.
Where can I go, Lord?
No one else has words that burn my heart.
No one else has words that fill the aching void.
Pretty words, yes. Beautiful, endearing words.
But not words that satisfy my longing soul.
Not words like "come unto me . . . I will give you rest."
Not words like "he leadeth me beside the still waters. . . ."

No one else can say, "My peace I give unto you."
For no one else can give peace.
Yes, Lord,
Your words are sometimes hard.
I do not always understand them,
And my soul does not always respond
In total abandon and surrender to Your words,
But they still are words of eternality,
Of joy, of peace, of all that makes life worth living.
Even when they are hard.
Thank You, Lord,
For the words that make my heart cry
"Abba . . . Father."

Lord,
The world's pull is constant,
Unrelenting and vicious,
Sometimes bold, sometimes subtle.
You have said I am not to love the world,
And if I do, the Father's love is not in me.
But what is loving the world, Lord?
It cannot mean I am not to love people,
For You love them and have told me to do so.
It cannot refer to the world of nature,
For You created that and called it good.
The world, then, must be a system.
A system that vies for my affection,
That seeks my attention
So that my heart and mind
Are diverted from You.
Righteousness is not abstinence
From a long list of things someone has said is wrong.
Abstinence may only focus attention
On the thing being avoided.
Nor does abstinence necessarily lessen the desire.
It may help build a resistance,
All the while, lurking underneath,
The thoughts are never put to rest.
Lord, teach us that worldliness
Is not so much an action as an attitude.
Worldliness is anything, good or bad, which
Spoils my spiritual experience of You,
Dulls my spiritual appetite for You,
Retards my spiritual growth in You,
Or threatens my spiritual influence with others.
Lord, grant that I may be so divorced from the world
That I find all my springs flow forth from You.

Father,
I thank You for freedom to be me with You.
I thank You that preachers can no longer intimidate me
Into being what I am not,
Or doing what I feel is cheapening or degrading
To my fellowship with You.
And it was a preacher, Lord,
Who forced me into this freedom.
I was tired but I had gone to church
To worship You and to receive strength from You.
The preacher suddenly said,
"Now we will take an attitude test."
And I had come to worship You.
"Raise your hands and say 'Praise the Lord,'" he continued.
Father, it is unnatural for me to do this in public,
Though in private I may do either or both.
I was perplexed!
Should I do an act of worship foreign to my nature,
Or dared I be myself?
Then he said, "If you can't raise your hands and say
'Praise the Lord,' you're backslidden."
That solved my problem.
I remember my victory when I said,
"You and I both know that is not true, Lord."
And without rancor or shame kept my hands in my lap.
In that moment peace and quietness came over me,
And I knew he could never again intimidate me.
Never again would I accept forms of worship
To please men. I would be myself.
Whether the preacher thought I was backslidden or not.
It no longer mattered what he thought,

For You and I were in fellowship.
We knew the freedom of love.
Thank You, Father,
And help that preacher to be free, too!

57.

Lord,
Will we ever get over the numbers syndrome?
"The bigger the better . . ."
"The more the merrier . . ."
Unless it's the most, it's not anything.
Such a spirit even carries over into our praying.
When a problem arises, tragedy strikes,
Or we just need an emotional uplift,
We think that by getting all our friends . . .
And the stronger saints . . .
To storm the doors of heaven,
Like some giant battering ram,
With their prayers,
We somehow can get You to change Your mind,
And, even if grudgingly, give us our requests.
As though the number of people praying
Would have any influence on You!
Or maybe, Lord,
We just feel someone else
Has Your attention a little more than do we.
O God! O God!
Won't we ever believe You are Love?
When will we learn Your ear is ever listening
For the faintest cry,
The softest sob,
The merest whimper
From Your "little ones"?
Thank You, Lord,
That we do not have to pray frantically,
Like the prophets of Baal.
Thank You that we do not have to clamour to get your attention.
Oh, Father, how could it be

That not even a sparrow can fall
Without your seeing and caring,
Yet You would not hear my plea?
Not so, Lord, for I am worth more than a sparrow,
And You *do* care for me.
Thank You for others who pray.
And thank You, Lord, that I can pray
In the quiet assurance
I need no "go-between,"
For Your heart hears even me when
My heart cries "Abba . . . Father."

58.

Father,
I don't mean to badger You,
Yet You have told me to ask,
And keep on asking.
Seek and knock.
It seems You mean for me to be persistent,
Even insistent.
I know that as my Father
It is Your delight and joy
Not only to hear, but to answer
The prayers of Your children.
How little we enter into that communion, Lord.
I do not want a "push-button" servant,
Nor an instant panacea.
I do not seek a miracle worker,
No, not even a deliverer.
I want, Lord,
A companion, a comforter,
One to fill the vacancies in my soul.
One to Whom I can speak,
Or one with whom I can weep
Without fear of being discovered or shamed.
Thank You, Father, that You are that One.
Thank You that I always have Your listening ear.
Because You love me,
And You are not waiting for me to prove my worth
Before You will listen.
I have no worth, but You love me anyway,
Because You are love.
I respond to that love, Father,
So I keep coming boldly, asking, seeking, and knocking.
If that is badgering,
So be it!

59

Lord,
Five years ago I could give the answer
To anything.
Just ask me.
Even without being asked
I often gave the answers
In my meek, humble way.
I knew how to solve problems.
If the problem were this, this was the answer.
It was all so pat,
And correct,
And rigid . . . and wrong.
Now, Lord,
I feel so ignorant, but so relieved.
How wonderfully liberating it is
Not to have to know all the answers.
It seems as though I were beginning again.
Fresh, simple, unwise . . . and free.
How fettered we become
By what we know.
How bound we become by dogma and doctrine.
How harsh, critical, and unloving we become
By being unmercifully right.
Lord, I knew what was right,
What was wrong,
And how stupid those were who did not know
As I knew.
Forgive, Lord, my self-righteousness.
Thank You, Lord,
For freedom from myself,
And liberty in You.

Now I do not have to know.
I can trust.
Thank You, Lord,
For emancipation.

60.

Lord,
Thank You for my Pastor.
In a day when so many are crying
For an able shepherd of the flock,
When so many are disappointed, brokenhearted,
And have lost faith in their spiritual leaders,
How blessed I am, Lord,
To have my Pastor.
This man, Lord, is a complete contrast
To the Madison Avenue hard sell, Mr. Personality
That most Pastors portray.
He is low keyed, having no need
For "hellfire and brimstone" messages,
For he knows and imparts to "the family" (as he calls us)
The grace, mercy, love, and peace of God.
He makes me to know that You care about me, Lord.
He is a man at peace with You and with himself,
Accepting not only himself, but others
Just as they are.
He lets me be human without feeling guilty about it.
He is a tough disciplinarian of himself
While being gentle with others.
He is a tender but firm man,
Humble but not weak,
Compassionate but not syrupy sweet,
Spiritual but not self-righteous.
He is a knowledgeable intellectual, but utterly simple.
He is a learned theologian, but never dull.
He seems to be totally unimpressed by, or ambitious for,
Position and power, fame or fortune.
He is a rugged man physically and spiritually,
Alive, alert, optimistic, and eager for life.

He imparts Your word with beauty and simplicity.
When he speaks, it is as if You are speaking.
He has taught me more about worship,
Real, honest heart worship,
Than has anyone else.
For this I am grateful.
For "the family" and for this man of God,
I thank You, Lord.

61.

Lord,
When it is six o'clock
In the morning of our lives,
Nine o'clock seems never to come.
Twelve o'clock is a dream.
Three o'clock will come to others, but not to us.
We avoid even thinking about the eleventh hour,
And the last hour is hidden in the dark recesses of the mind.
But the clock ticks on,
Unrelentingly, unhesitatingly, unmercifully,
Never stopping even for a moment's rest.
The early morning hours, like the morning dew,
Are clean and refreshing, innocent and joyous.
Each minute adds to our life's day
Until the responsibilities of noontime,
The shock of midafternoon
Jar us into the reality that the clock
Is headed downhill,
Swiftly and surely.
All our yearning for the setting of the clock
To an earlier hour
Are vain hopes,
Dashed by every precise tick.
No wonder, Lord,
You told us to number our days.
We always think there is still enough time.
Later I will . . . later . . . later . . .
It *is* later now, Lord.
Thank You that every day has its reward.
Even the hoaryheaded eleventh hour.
But most of all, thank You for the final hour
When absence becomes presence,

When death is swallowed up in victory.
We no longer see through a glass darkly,
But face to face,
And faith becomes glorious sight.